Anonymous

Valedictory address of His Excellency Alexander H. Bullock,

To the two branches of the legislature of Massachusetts, January 7, 1869

Anonymous

Valedictory address of His Excellency Alexander H. Bullock,
To the two branches of the legislature of Massachusetts, January 7, 1869

ISBN/EAN: 9783337727666

Printed in Europe, USA, Canada, Australia, Japan

Cover: Foto ©ninafisch / pixelio.de

More available books at **www.hansebooks.com**

VALEDICTORY ADDRESS

OF

HIS EXCELLENCY

ALEXANDER H. BULLOCK,

TO THE

TWO BRANCHES

OF THE

Legislature of Massachusetts,

JANUARY 7, 1869.

BOSTON:

WRIGHT & POTTER, STATE PRINTERS,

79 MILK STREET, (CORNER OF FEDERAL.)

1869.

ADDRESS.

Gentlemen of the Senate,

    and of the House of Representatives:

Before transferring to an eminent citizen of the
Commonwealth the labors and responsibilities of the
office to which he has been summoned by his fellow
citizens in a manner which marks their appreciation
of his private virtues and his public services, I deem
it proper to communicate with the Legislature concerning several matters of grave import, affecting the
moral and material interests of Massachusetts. Impressed with the duty of the Chief Magistrate to
impart, and the right of the people to receive, the
fullest and most precise information respecting the
public business, I have the honor to present such information in detail upon some of the measures which

have been initiated, have progressed, or been matured
during my official term. I have the honor to transmit at the same time, for the information of the
Legislature, several reports of public officers, and
other documents which merit the attention and may
require the action of the General Court.

THE PUBLIC FINANCE.

A brief review of the financial results of the last
three years will commend itself to the attention and
thoughtful consideration of the tax-paying citizens of
the Commonwealth.

At the commencement of my official term the nation
had just emerged from a long and costly war, which
had entailed upon Massachusetts a heavy burden of
indebtedness already accrued, with the inevitable contingency of a large prospective increase under the
operation of various acts of special legislation rendered necessary by the exigencies of the conflict. It
should also be remembered that, in response to the
demands of public enterprise, charity and education,
Massachusetts has in this period, as before, generously maintained her reputation, bestowing her
munificence with unprecedented liberality.

The result is strikingly apparent in the fact, that,
while the floating or unfunded liabilities of the State

have been reduced but little more than three millions of dollars since 1866, (amounting at the present time to nine hundred twenty-eight thousand dollars,) the funded debt has been enlarged upwards of seven millions during the same period, a net increase of more than two millions having occurred within the last year.

Among the causes directly and indirectly contributing to this result may be enumerated the following:—

First, the large disbursements required for the liquidation of State bounties remaining unpaid at the close of the war, the aggregate amount paid from the beginning being nearly four and a half millions of dollars in excess of the scrip issued for that purpose; second, the continuance of State aid to the families and dependents of Massachusetts Volunteers, the re-imbursement of which to cities and towns swells to an aggregate of three and three-quarters millions of dollars for the years 1866–7–8; third, the heavy drafts upon the treasury for the prosecution of the Troy and Greenfield Railroad and Hoosac Tunnel enterprise, for which, during the four years previous to 1868, nearly three millions of dollars in excess of the issue of scrip have been advanced from the proceeds of temporary loans and from the ordinary revenues of the Commonwealth, to which might be added another half million

of dollars since advanced on the same account and in
the same manner; fourth, the largely increased interest on the public debt, and the high premium on gold,
both amounting in the aggregate to an annual average
of one million four hundred and fifty thousand dollars; fifth, the extraordinary expenditures authorized
by acts of special legislation in excess of previous estimates,—in some cases but partially provided for, and in
others not even considered, in the basis of taxation,—
*amounting in a single year to more than eight hundred
thousand dollars, and during the three years mentioned
to more than one and a half millions of dollars ;* sixth,
the loan in aid of the Boston, Hartford and Erie Railroad, authorized by the Legislature of 1867.

From an intelligent estimate of these heavy aggregates and the causes of their accumulation it will be
easy to understand how rapidly a public debt may
stride into very large proportions. The following tabulated statement exhibits these financial results in a
clear and comprehensive form :—

Funded debt, Jan. 1, 1866,   .   .$19,056,435 56
Unfunded debt, Jan. 1, 1866, .   . 4,177,196 19
                                   _____
     Total, ...$23,233,631 75

Funded debt, Jan. 1, 1869, . . $26,807,420 00
Unfunded debt, Jan. 1, 1869, . . 928,450 05
                                  _____
        Total, ... $27,735,870 05

Increase of funded debt, . . . $7,750,984 44
Decrease of unfunded debt, . . 3,248,746 14
                                  _____
Showing a net increase of the aggre-
    gate debt, during the three years, of $4,502,238 30

From this comparative statement of the funded liabilities of the Commonwealth, is deducted that portion
which has been liquidated on maturity during years
named, amounting to $2,859,900, and there remains
the net increase as above stated, which has accumulated from the following issues of scrip :—

For the Bounty Fund Loan, . . $1,951,244 00
For Massachusetts War Loan, . . 3,505,000 00
Troy and Greenfield Railroad and
    Hoosac Tunnel Loan, . . . 2,952,400 00
Western Railroad Loan, . . . 1,510,080 00
Hartford and Erie Railroad Loan, . 290,400 00

Redemption of the Funded Debt.

It should be borne in mind that, while the foregoing statement indicates a large increase of the public
debt, the available assets applicable to its redemption
have proportionably accumulated; so that, in a strictly
financial view, the pecuniary condition of the Commonwealth has rarely, if ever, exhibited a more gratifying and creditable aspect.

In substantial conformity with recommendations
communicated in my last annual message, for the
retirement or payment of existing unfunded loans
and liabilities, and the establishment of additional
sinking funds from resources already available and
at our disposal, for the redemption of the funded
loans without resort to further taxation for that
purpose, the Legislature of 1868 made ample provision for the payment of nearly six millions of
liabilities, including the Coast Defence Loan and
the new Loan in aid of the Troy and Greenfield
Railroad and Hoosac Tunnel.

As the result of that legislation, almost three millions of dollars previously advanced from temporary
loans and from the ordinary revenue, in anticipation
of the sale of scrip, have been restored to the common
uses of the treasury; while the payment at maturity
of all but $352,000 of the entire funded loan is now

fully secured by well-endowed sinking funds, which, with their legitimate accumulations, will be ample for that purpose, without the unwelcome contingency of taxation. For the payment of the small amount thus unprovided for by specific legislation, most of it maturing in 1870–72, the surplusage of funds already established will be much more than sufficient.

The Massachusetts Funds and their Securities.

In connection with the subject of finance, every tax-payer will be especially gratified to know that the securities in which the funds are invested, a very large proportion of them being Massachusetts bonds, possess a market value nearly one-sixth more than their cost. The assets belonging to the seventeen Sinking and Trust Funds of the State amount to more than twelve millions of dollars, and the aggregate market value of their securities exceeds the amount of original investments by *nearly one million eight hundred thousand dollars.*

The several Sinking Funds *applicable to the redemption of the Funded Debt* already amount in the aggregate to *nine and a half millions of dollars*—considerably more than one-third of the entire debt. When it is considered that the maturing of this debt is graded over intervals extending onward for more than thirty years, it will be at once seen that these funds, with their natural accumulations, cannot fail to become in the aggregate largely in excess of the amount actually required for liquidation. Besides, the securities in which they are invested have at the present time a market value of *more than one and a quarter millions of dollars above the original investment or cost.*

Assuredly, in view of this largely enhanced value of its bonds, unusual if not unprecedented in the history of States, every citizen of Massachusetts may cherish pride in its financial credit at home and abroad. Our bonds, of which the payment of both principal and interest in gold is sacredly guarantied and unerringly fulfilled, command everywhere a confidence not surpassed in the commerce of the globe.

STATE LOAN TO BOSTON, HARTFORD AND ERIE RAILROAD COMPANY.

By chapter 284 of the acts of the year 1867, a State loan of three millions of dollars was made to the Boston, Hartford and Erie Railroad Company, to enable it to complete its road to the Hudson River. The absolute granting or delivery of this subsidy was by the act made contingent upon the fulfilment of certain conditions which should be made to appear

to the satisfaction of the Governor and Council, of
the Attorney-General, and of certain commissioners
to be appointed under the sixth section. I deemed
it fortunate for the State, that upon this commission
I was enabled to procure the services of Messrs.
George T. Bigelow, Emory Washburn and Samuel
Ashburner.

The Commissioners, after long and thorough investigation, made an extended report upon the whole
subject, and in conclusion expressed the opinion that,
if the means and resources of the company should
be honestly and judiciously used, and with a reason-
able degree of energy, enterprise and economy, the
road might be thereby constructed and moderately
equipped, and they accordingly recommended the
allowance by the Governor and Council of a loan
of scrip for the work already done and equipment
purchased. A copy of this report is herewith communicated. This document was transmitted to the
Attorney-General, with the request that he would
report upon the various matters in which his concurrent action was required. A copy of his reply is
also transmitted.

It was quite obvious to my mind that it was the
design of the Legislature to secure the separate and
responsible judgment of the Governor and Council

upon each of the particulars named in the act as
necessary to be shown. It also became early apparent that the principal questions concerning which
doubts would exist, were, whether the requirements
of the statute concerning the payment and cancella-
tion of the mortgage debts secured by the underlying mortgages on that part of the road this side
of Southbridge and Willimantic had been complied
with, and whether the company had satisfactorily
shown that they would be able, without further aid
from this Commonwealth, to complete their line from
Boston to Fishkill before May 27, 1872.

Deeply impressed with the responsibility imposed
upon me in respect to these questions, I gave my
careful and personal attention to the examination of
the details which could throw light upon them.

A considerable discrepancy was found to exist in
the various statements of the outstanding bonds which
are secured by the underlying mortgages. This discrepancy was largely relieved by subsequent explanations; and a bond with personal sureties was required,
in the penal sum of one million of dollars, to protect
the franchise and property described in the Berdell
mortgage from the uncancelled bonds, thus dispensing
with the necessity of a precise ascertainment of the

number of bonds outstanding, which indeed seemed impracticable.

The Committee of the Council, to whom I referred the question, became satisfied that the company will be able to complete their line of road to Fishkill within the time specified by the act, without further aid from this Commonwealth, as appears by their report, a copy of which is herewith submitted. Wishing, however, rigidly to test the conclusion to which the Committee of the Council had come upon this latter subject, I addressed to the Commissioners a supplementary communication, which expressed the doubts that still remained in my mind, and the want of full information, which, as it seemed to me, still existed, upon certain facts bearing upon the question; and a copy of this communication, and of the reply of the Commissioners, is also herewith sent to the Legislature.

By this reply, the validity of the acceptances of the Erie Railroad did not appear to be established, and I was not able quite to concur with the opinion of the Commissioners that it would seem a fair estimate to offset the accruing interest money, which the company would apparently be obliged to pay, against the earnings of the road. Up to this time it had been assumed that the full period allowed by the act for the completion of the road to Fishkill might be occupied in doing the work. It was obvious that an amount of about $3,000,000 would become due for interest before the end of that period. By the last exhibit of the Commissioners, the sums to be paid by the company exceeded their pecuniary resources, now within their control. There were also certain other matters of detail concerning which I desired further information. I therefore presented certain inquiries to the officers of the company, a copy of which, and of their replies thereto, and of an accompanying opinion of Mr. William M. Evarts is transmitted to you.

By these replies, it appeared that it is the purpose of the company nearly or quite to complete their line of road to Fishkill during the present year; and, upon personal conference with Mr. Ashburner, one of the Commissioners, himself a civil engineer of large experience in this kind of work, I became satisfied that this may be done. This early completion of the road will greatly diminish the amount of interest to be paid.

This opinion of Mr. Evarts was submitted to the Attorney-General, and he deemed it satisfactory to establish the liability of the Erie Railroad Company for the bonds which they have received. But it should now be stated that the acceptances of the Erie Com-

·pany have since been anticipated by the cash payment of the whole amount.

Upon the whole case, as thus presented, the question then remained, what rule should be adopted as a guide by which to determine whether the company will be able to complete their line of road to Fishkill without further aid from the Commonwealth? Were they to be required to demonstrate mathematically an actual present ability, from means now within their control, to meet the necessary disbursements? Or, would they meet the requirement of the statute by making it appear to the satisfaction of the reason and conscience that in all human probability they will be able to accomplish the work? Accepting the latter as the true rule, bearing in mind the valuation which the public have now for a long time put upon the shares of the company, and believing that this indicates the existence of a borrowing capacity on the part of the company yet remaining, which is equal to the difference· between the required disbursements and their present actual means, I felt constrained to grant the first instalments of the loan in accordance with the certificate of the Commissioners. Five hundred thousand dollars expressed in sterling bonds have accordingly been already delivered.

My individual judgment is adverse to the practice

which has sprung up of late years in the Legislature
of granting large sums of money conditioned upon the
discretionary action of the Governor and Council. It
may well be doubted whether in some instances of this
kind the Executive Department has not been charged
with a trust of finance which belongs peculiarly to the
Legislature. However that may be, acting under a
responsibility to execute the law, and after an amount
of time, care and thought bestowed upon this case
which is by no means represented in the brief terms
of the present statement, I have seen my way and duty
to consummate this loan. I think it proper that the
papers relating to the question should be made known
to the Legislature; and I have confidence that the
progress and completion of the road, and its future
working operations, will sustain the result I have
reached, and confirm my opinion of its importance in
the commercial interests of the Commonwealth.

DISEASE IN CATTLE.

During the past season a considerable degree of
interest, at times amounting almost to general con-
cern, has been awakened by the appearance of a mal-
ady among the cattle. Its most marked development
has been in Texas or Cherokee beeves; but these,
when transported to the North and East in the spring

and summer months, have endangered the kind in all the States exposed by their transit and stay. Acting in co-operation with the Executive heads of many of the States, and in compliance with the request of some of our own citizens most intelligent in the subject, I appointed Commissioners to have charge of the field of inquiry, and to see to the enforcement of the laws provided for such cases. So inadequate as to the compensation of the Commissioners are the provisions of chapter twenty-eight of the acts of 1862, under which alone such appointment could be made, that I found it impracticable to obtain the services of any person upon the commission whose scientific or professional studies peculiarly fitted him for this particular investigation. In a matter so profoundly interesting in its relations to political and domestic economy, affecting directly the property and health of the people, the limitations of the statute in effect deprived the State of the official service of a reputable physician or veterinary surgeon. But the good will and patriotic spirit of two men of practical wisdom enabled me to so far organize the commission as to keep watch at the frontier points of delivery of cattle to our railroads, and, generally, to protect our markets and herds.

Late in the autumn I further appointed Dr. E. F.

3

Thayer, a veterinary surgeon of approved repute, to represent this Commonwealth in a convention of Commissioners from several States, held in Springfield, Illinois, for the consideration of the whole subject. Twelve States were represented in this assembly, whose deliberations resulted in the approval of a series of measures to be recommended to the Legislatures of the States. These will be found contained in the report of the Commissioner, which is now transmitted to the General Court.

CAPE COD HARBOR.

In my last annual message I expressed my readiness to approve the plan of the Commissioners for the protection and preservation of the harbor at Provincetown so soon as the Legislature should enlarge the appropriation sufficiently to meet the estimate of cost. A further appropriation of fifty thousand dollars was made; and I have now the pleasure to communicate to the General Court the complete success of the undertaking.

The protection and preservation of Cape Cod Harbor, so important to the State and nation, has been a subject of interest for many years. The United States Engineers have given it their attention from time to time since the first military survey by Col.

J. D. Graham in 1833–4–5, and various works
have been undertaken there, mostly, however, of
small proportions. Col. Graham called the attention
of the Government to the importance of closing up
East Harbor Inlet, and pointed out the danger of the
ocean breaking through the low and narrow gaps in
the outside beach at the " head of the meadows."
Various Boards of United States Engineers and State
Commissioners have examined and reported these
sources of danger, and plans have been proposed for
closing the Inlet of East Harbor ; one for a strong
stone dike of double walls filled in with sand, and
one for a dike of loaded crib work.

Circumstances, however, seem to have prevented
action in regard to any of these proposed improvements, until, in the opinion of those most familiar
with it, the condition of the Harbor became so critical
that a Special Board of State Commissioners was
appointed, with an eminent hydraulic engineer, Mr.
James B. Francis, as its chairman, for the purpose of
devising practical means for the " protection and
preservation " of the Harbor.

As a basis for study and action, this Board called
upon Prof. Benjamin Peirce, Superintendent of the
United States Coast Survey, for a thorough survey
of the ground in question, in order to show, by com-

parison with the survey of Col. Graham, the character and extent of the changes which thirty-two years had effected. This survey was executed by Assistant H. L. Whiting of the Coast Survey, and showed conclusively that changes injurious to the Harbor had occurred and were progressing. To prevent these injuries it became necessary to close the Inlet of East Harbor.

It should be noted that this Inlet was a powerful tidal water-way more than a thousand feet in width, through which the column of the tide of Massachusetts Bay, ranging from nine to sixteen feet in height, rushed in and out, filling and emptying " East Harbor "—a lagoon containing an area of one thousand acres at high tides. The material of the sides and bottom of this Inlet was coarse, loose sand, affording no foundation for any solid structure. Closing this Inlet and stopping a water-way far more powerful than that of either the Connecticut or Merrimack Rivers, at Springfield or Lowell, was a problem of great uncertainty, and the case a novel one in the history of our coast or harbor improvement or river damming.

The plan of the structure prepared by Mr. Francis was the result of careful examination and profound study, and involved an estimated expenditure of

$149,134.80. The act making this appropriation was passed by the Legislature on the 19th of May, and the plans of the Commissioners were at once approved by the Governor and Council. As no contracts or other definite arrangements could be made until after the act of appropriation, a short working season was left for the Commissioners to collect material and concentrate forces at East Harbor. Active operations were commenced there on the 26th of June, and on the 4th of November the Inlet was successfully and permanently closed.

The work which has produced this important result is a timber dam of great strength and perfection. A foundation for this structure had to be created. This was done by double rows of sheet piling, driven from twelve to fourteen feet into the sand, then cut off just above the bottom surface of the channel and heavily planked over, to prevent the water, in its pressure, from bursting through the treacherous material beneath the structure and undermining it. Guard wings were also built on either side of the Inlet, with sheet-piling driven equally deep and carried far up into the sandy shores above high water.

So complete have been all parts of this structure that not an accident or an interruption has occurred during its progress, nor a single fault, which, if al-

lowed, might have involved the failure of the whole
work. When all was ready, on November 4th, the
main superstructure of the timber dam was shut down
—like an immense water-gate—during the period of
one tide. All that now remains to be done is to fill in
sand, in accordance with the original plan, covering
the whole wooden structure and forming a dike as
solid and permanent as the shore and beach on either
side of it. About one thousand cubic yards of sand
are now filling in per day, at which rate the embank-
ment will be completed in a few months.

The character and proportions of this work may
be better understood by stating that it contains about
one million feet of lumber; that three thousand piles
have been driven in the sand, most of them to an
unusual depth in such material. Twenty tons of
iron have been used, and six thousand tons of
stone,—the latter as a guard to prevent the tear-
ing action of the water through the sand. A large
number of sand bags have also been used for the
same purpose, and many more held in reserve. This
structure, which has closed East Harbor Inlet, is
altogether worthy of the reputation of Mr. Francis,
the engineer who planned it. Although somewhat
remote from his accustomed field of labor, every
condition of success, as well as every danger, was

anticipated. The estimates were made with such precision as almost exactly to coincide with the actual outlay.

Before any work was undertaken at East Harbor, Mr. Francis resigned his connection with the Commission, and Mr. Paul Hill was appointed in his place. Great credit is due to the untiring zeal and energy of this gentleman, under whose immediate direction the work has been principally conducted. By his rapid execution, and rare ability to meet every emergency, he has prevented any waste of the money of the State. The other members of the Board, General R. A. Pierce, and Mr. James Gifford, have shared in this spirit and action, and the labors of this Commission have not only been prosecuted with great energy and complete success, but with an economy quite unusual in works undertaken by the State. And we may expect here the unusual gratification of an important work costing less than its appropriation by a margin of between twenty-five and thirty thousand dollars—over sixteen per cent.

Important work has been done by the General Government during the last six months, under the able supervision of General J. G. Foster, of the U. S. Engineers, in addition to works previously constructed for the preservation of the Harbor.

At Beach Point, an extensive bulkhead of brush
has been constructed, extending from the termina-
tion of the old wooden bulkhead to the extremity of
the bridge across East Harbor Inlet—a distance of
one thousand feet—having along its whole length
jetties fifty feet apart and fifty feet in length. The
construction of the bulkhead and jetties, being of
brush interlaced around and between rows of pickets
driven firmly into the sand and weighted with layers
of stone interspersed throughout the mass of brush,
has made the most admirable and effective beach
protection that has ever been provided for these
wasting shores. Its adaptation to the case in question is already manifest by the accumulation of sand
upon the shore of Beach Point. General Foster
intends to extend this bulkhead to the southward
over the site of the former wooden structure, and
also, if necessary, to extend it northward, and unite
it with the Commissioners' Dike.

As there appeared well-grounded apprehension
that the encroachment of the ocean upon the outer
beach opposite the head of the meadows would
result in the sea breaking through the narrow ridge
of sand in some great storm, it was decided by General Foster to construct a substantial dike across
the meadow at the "wading place"—opposite High

Head—so that even if a break should occur in the outer beach, the sea would come no farther towards the harbor.

Upon Long Point, near the light-house, about one thousand tons of stone have been uniformly distributed along the beach, and, with the stone previously placed there, serve as an efficient protection against the abrasion of the waves and currents upon the shore.

An excellent understanding exists between the U. S. Engineer in charge—General Foster—and the Engineers and Commissioners of the State, leading to a cordial co-operation in all plans and works calculated to improve and protect this important Harbor. And I desire to express a public obligation to Professor Peirce, to his Assistant, Mr. Henry L. Whiting, and to General Foster, for the prompt and efficient assistance which they have constantly rendered.

I have thought it advisable to explain this work somewhat in detail on account of its intrinsic importance, and especially in order that full information as to the subject may be at hand in an official form whenever the State shall call upon the federal government for re-imbursement, as contemplated in the original act of appropriation passed in 1867.

4

I have the honor to lay before you two communications, dated respectively November 25th and December 11th, from the State Agent at Washington, Lieut. Col. Gardiner Tufts, setting forth succinctly what has been accomplished since the close of the war in settling our military claims against the United States. Until the beginning of the year 1867 the preparation and presentation of our accounts for these claims was under charge of the Auditor of the Commonwealth. In February of that year I withdrew this business from that office, and have caused it to be conducted since under my own supervision. During the administration of my predecessor five different accounts, for the aggregate sum of $3,501,766.50, had been presented against the United States. Of this sum, when I came to the executive office, there were suspended or disallowed items to the amount of $946,006.76, and none of these suspensions or disallowances had been revoked. My first measure was to commit the accounts, with all the papers appertaining to them, to Colonel A. G. Browne, Jr., the military secretary of my predecessor, to examine them critically, and report what in his opinion could be accomplished towards removing the objections raised by the United States, and the best mode for doing so;

with instructions to consult with me personally from
time to time in the progress of his investigation. This
task occupied Colonel Browne for several months, and
in August, 1867, he made a report advising that all
but a comparatively inconsiderable portion of the
items suspended or disallowed could be reinforced by
such additional proofs and explanations, as, under the
amended rules of the accounting officers of the United
States, would procure the withdrawal of the objections. And he recommended that the business of
preparing these proofs and explanations, (many of
which, from his acquaintance with our military administration during the war, he was himself able to
suggest,) should be intrusted to some special officer
who should be able to superintend it here and also to
present them personally at Washington. This rec-
ommendation concurring with my own judgment, I
selected and detailed for that duty, Lieut. Col. Tufts,
whose reports above referred to show the gratifying
result that out of the amount of $946,006.76 disal-
lowed or suspended on those five accounts, $932,113.77
(or more than 98½ per cent.,) have been allowed and
collected during the year 1868; and also that, on a
sixth account for $33,498.29, prepared and presented
during the year, $31,502.79 have been allowed by the
third auditor. The success which these figures indi-

cate is the best evidence of the intelligence, discretion and fidelity with which the work has been executed. And I may add with propriety that it confirms in a most satisfactory manner not only the fact that our military expenditures in behalf of the United States during the war were made with scrupulous integrity and, excellent judgment, but also the fact that our accounts were kept with corresponding skill and accuracy. The entire expense to the Commonwealth of these protracted and voluminous proceedings has been only about one-half of one per cent. of the amount recovered. In this service, distinguished not more by the result than by the industry and fidelity which accomplished it, the labors of Col. Browne, Lieut. Col. Tufts and Mr. Julius L. Clarke have been conspicuous.

BOUNTIES—PAST AND FUTURE.

Under my order, the Bureau of the Paymaster was closed in February last. From the passage of the bounty laws to January 1st, 1869, the whole amount of payments made may be stated as follows:—

Advance—Army, . . .	$9,595,150 00
" Navy, . . .	83,098 70
Monthly, ...	3,073,217 04
	$12,751,465 74

There is a considerable amount of unpaid bounties and claims which should for the most part be treated as doubtful or fraudulent, and classified as follows:— 1st. Bounties apparently due—the soldier's record being clear, but no application for the amount having been made by him or by his heirs. The amount of this class is small. 2d. Doubtful claims—in which cases the evidence of enlistment or service is incomplete, and, if the missing evidence be supplied, the bounty would become due. 3d. Improper and fraudulent claims. This class would include men who enlisted, and, being incapable of performing service, were discharged without United States pay, but who claim the State bounty; and bounties of deserters, claimed by agents holding orders from the soldiers, and who advanced, or profess to have advanced the bounty before desertion.

It is estimated that these amount altogether to a total of about $370,000.

Although the amount of bounties really due, or which will become due in the future by the required evidence being supplied, will not probably exceed $25,000 or $30,000, the State might be made liable for a large part of the foregoing estimate by relaxing its watchfulness, or by unwise legislation opening the

door for the payment of any of these improper or
fraudulent claims.

To guard the Treasury against such exposure, at
the close of the past year I issued an order directing
that bounty claims shall first be submitted to a commission appointed by the Governor for investigation,
and that, if found to be justly due, they shall, upon
the approval of a majority of the Commissioners, be
allowed and paid upon new rolls vouched and approved according to the orders heretofore issued by
the Executive. I beg leave to remind the General
Court that so well preserved, classified and understood
are the records of this department, that rarely can a
just claim come to the Legislature on appeal from
rejection by the Executive. The danger of inconsid-
erate liberality towards this class of cases will increase
as time shall elapse.

I transmit a communication from that excellent
officer, the late Paymaster, Mr. William H. Porter,
relative to the condition of the records of his department. The names of all the soldiers appearing upon
pay-rolls are now registered, forty-two thousand in
number, so arranged that for the purpose of reference
the index is now complete. When the work shall be
finished, the books will be indispensable, not only for
reference to the original vouchers, but as ledgers giv-

ing the bounty account of each soldier. Completed, they will exhibit a system as nearly perfect as that of any government; and, for the amount of bounties paid and for the manner of their payment to the soldiers of Massachusetts, they cannot fail to warrant the patriotic pride of every citizen.

THE INLAND FISHERIES.

There is one feature of the official transactions of the last three years which relates to the development of a branch of industry allied to agriculture, of special value in point of view both of science and practical use. I refer to the labors of the Commissioners who have had in charge the re-establishment and protection of inland fisheries. Although the deep-sea fisheries have always been regarded as a productive source of wealth and power, encouraged by bounties and protected by treaties, yet, until within a very recent period, the profit and advantage of stocking our own streams had never been realized or even estimated. In 1856 Commissioners were appointed by the Legislature to investigate the subject of artificially propagating fish; but their labors ended in a few experiments and a report. Nearly ten years passed before attention was again attracted to the subject by the complaints of New Hampshire and

Vermont of the damage we had done to their fisheries by artificial dams on the Merrimack and the Connecticut. In our efforts to encourage manufactures, we had thoughtlessly barricaded those great rivers against the ascent of fish. The propriety and justice of these complaints was recognized at once; and, in April 1865, the appointment of commissioners, Mr. Theodore Lyman and Mr. A. A. Reed, was authorized to investigate them, whose report, rendered in December 1865, created an interest in the subjects which it treated as universal as had been the previous ignorance or indifference. It set forth clearly the quantity of fish formerly taken in those rivers, the diminution of it through obstructions and pollutions of the water, the method of constructing fishways, and the natural history of the salmon, the shad and other valuable fishes, which once abounded in our streams; and explained how the work of re-stocking must be of gradual progress, from which few results popularly appreciable could be counted on in less than five years.

In May 1866, the appointment of the present board of commissioners (Mr. Lyman and Mr. A. R. Field,) was authorized by the General Court, and a small appropriation made for river improvements, to be expended under their direction. Before the begin

ning of the next year, through the cordial co-operation
of the mill-owners of Lawrence and Lowell, the
Merrimack was opened by fishways; and (what was
more important,) general attention was drawn to, and
public interest excited in, the methods for re-stocking
not only that river, but all our streams and ponds.
By the laws of 1867, the general powers of the
Commissioners were enlarged, authority was given
to them to cause fishways to be built over all dams,
and to re-stock ponds as well as rivers, and the
fishing for shad or salmon in the Merrimack was
prohibited for five years. During the remainder of
that year they gave special attention to the artificial
propagation of fish, and the report which they
rendered a year ago stimulated in a most gratifying
manner the interest of the community in that branch
of the general subject. On the Connecticut the breed-
ing of shad, by the processes described, was undertaken on a large scale. On the Merrimack large
numbers of shad were taken into the waters above
the dams, and left to breed there naturally. But, in
regard to the building of fishways during the year,
the mill-owners of Holyoke, on the Connecticut,
being called upon to follow the example of those of
Lowell and Lawrence on the Merrimack, showed
themselves not moved by the same public spirit, and

even threw obstructions in the way of the Commissioners, to which I asked the attention of the Legislature of 1868, who voted an appropriation to make a fishway over the dam at Hadley's Falls, in case the water-power company should not be liable to build it. The Commissioners' report for 1868, which I have the honor herewith to lay before you, sets forth fully their present relations with that company. The fishway has not been built, for reasons which are there stated, and to which I ask your especial attention, since we owe to New Hampshire and Vermont an explanation of the causes of delay.

I beg, also, your consideration of all the lesser points on which the Commissioners suggest the expediency of legislation, among which they mention the need of protecting the white perch in the same manner as the smelt, and of amending all statutes which now protect pickerel, so as on the contrary to hold out inducements to destroy them; and particularly the need of co-operative legislation with Connecticut to check the indiscriminate slaughter of young shad by the pound-fisheries. That State has already passed a statute on the subject, limited to take effect on the passage of a similar act by Massachusetts. And to the further recommendations of the Commissioners for a general revisal of all our statutes on the subject of inland fisheries, for the withdrawal, so far as the Legislature may have power to do so, of the public privilege of free fishing in the rivers and great ponds, and for the enactment of laws giving to the raisers of fish some measure of the security of their rights of property which we afford to the raisers of other live stock, I beg your earnest and favorable attention. The need of all this is so fully and simply expressed by the Commissioners themselves, that I have only occasion to add that I am personally convinced of the wisdom, policy and expediency of all the measures which they urge, as demanded for the advancement of a branch of industry which promises a great and certain increase of domestic comfort, private wealth and public revenue.

I cannot leave this topic without adding what will meet from no one with more cordial concurrence than from his fellow commissioners, that what has been accomplished in this new and important field is due chiefly to Mr. Lyman, who, working with a rare combination of enthusiasm and persistency, has already gained results which are no less gratifying to the political economist than to the natural philosopher.

THE DEPARTMENT OF CHARITIES.

The work of the Department of the Charities, Reforms and Corrections, in the extent and variety of its details, exceeds that of any other Bureau of the State government. Official duty and personal interest have combined to lead me to a close examination of the system which controls them, both as originally adopted and as modified by successive Legislatures, and to a continuous observation of its workings. As the result, I have assured myself that this system was well adapted to the needs of the Commonwealth at the time of its establishment, and that the alterations necessitated by exigencies then unforeseen have been devised in a spirit of judicious liberality. I find, of course, defects, some of which are inherent and inevitable in any system, and cannot be entirely obviated by excellence of administration ; and others which doubtless are but temporary, and for which future legislators will unquestionably provide, whenever they are persuaded that the remedies suggested are sound and feasible. It is too much to expect that any code of law, or any organization under the law, designed to remedy human imperfections, will itself be perfect. But when faith in humanity is combined, in its advisory and executive officers, with intelligence and high culture, with a matured judgment, strong will, and resolute fidelity of performance, we can confidently look for an abatement of some immediate evils, and for a future solution of many difficult problems in the treatment of the pauper, the lunatic, and the criminal.

Such a supervision I am convinced that we enjoy, and that the State has been peculiarly fortunate in the wisdom of the Legislature of 1863, which, after thorough investigation and discussion, created the Board of State Charities. In the high character and ability of its successive chairmen, Otis Norcross and Dr. Samuel G. Howe, in the industry, energy and great ability of its secretary and general agent, whose retirement from office is a most serious loss to the Commonwealth and to humanity, and in the working capacity and the honesty of its subordinate officers, has been found an example of that combination above alluded to, which has wrought remarkable results. Though subjected to harsh criticism and unreasonable opposition, proceeding mainly from those unfamiliar with its specialty, or from interested parties affected by its measures of reform ; and though hampered by delay in obtaining much-needed legislation, it has advanced quietly in its work till it has remodelled the whole arrangement of our charities. Retaining whatever experience had proved to be good under the former supervision, it has abated many existing evils, cut off excrescences, introduced a successful classification, and, replacing jealousies between institutions with cordiality and willingness of co-operation, has greatly promoted their internal discipline, as well as the economy of their management. On referring to its record, I find among many other measures of utility the following which I deem it fitting to mention.

It has brought about the closing of the needless and expensive hospital at Rainsford Island, and inaugurated a system of providing for the sick poor of the State in their respective localities, with partial or complete re-imbursement to the cities and towns from the Treasury of the Commonwealth,—a policy dictated alike by justice and humanity.

It has effected an extension of the laws of settlement, thereby preventing hundreds of surviving soldiers and of the widows and orphans of the dead from being driven to the State Almshouses, and so has probably rendered needless for years to come the creation of any more large public institutions.

It has provided agents to visit the thousands of children apprenticed from our Almshouses and Reformatories, many of whom had formerly been grossly defrauded and abused without remedy or protection. It has carried through the establishment of the State Workhouse at Bridgewater for the restraint and employment of the vicious and vagrant poor, thereby nearly superseding the almshouse on the same premises. Under the able and judicious management of the superintendent, Mr. Goodspeed, this experiment is proving a complete success, not only in controlling but in preventing voluntary pauperism, in preserving infant life, and compelling some pecuniary return to the Commonwealth for the burden thrown upon its Treasury by idleness and vice.

It has put in operation the State Primary School at Monson, by which agency hundreds of children are relieved of the disabilities of pauperism, removed from the exceptional classes, and restored to society as profitable producers instead of dependent consumers.

It has secured the establishment of the Lunatic Asylum on the premises of the State at Tewksbury, for the reception of the chronic insane, thus relieving the Commonwealth from the erection and maintenance of a new Lunatic Hospital, and providing remunerative employment for large numbers of the insane.

It has collected and collated a vast amount of statistical information, undervalued perhaps by too many at home, but eagerly sought for and made the basis of legislative action by other communities.

In the five years of its existence, its officers have
examined more than 50,000 immigrants and 20,000
paupers; have removed from the State or otherwise
provided for 10,000 paupers, including 550 lunatics,
(or enough to fill two additional hospitals,) most of
whom would have been permanently chargeable, and
has paid into the Treasury more than $131,000.

While effecting these wholesome reforms, the
Board has done nothing to increase the number of
public dependents, for the average in our institutions has decreased 13 per cent. within the five years
of its existence; neither has it made any undue draft
upon the Treasury, for its collections have covered
its expenses, leaving a large surplus; while the total
expenditure of the State for the past year, in the
department of pauperism and lunacy, will not reach
$300,000, and, reducing currency to gold, does not
exceed the annual outlay of twelve years ago.

In my annual message for 1867, I had the honor to
recommend that provision be made within our own
limits for the education of the deaf-mutes of the Commonwealth. Regarding this suggestion with favor, the
Legislature of that year incorporated the Clarke Institution for Deaf-mutes, located at Northampton. Through
the munificence of the patron and constant friend
whose name it bears, and with but moderate assist-

ance from the State, it was put in operation in October of the same year, under the charge of an enthusiastic and self-sacrificing lady, whom I mention for the sake of honor,—Miss Harriet B. Rogers. Several visits, induced at first by a sense of personal responsibility, have awakened my deepest interest in its welfare. The method of articulation, which is there used to the exclusion of all others, was not regarded by experts with unanimous favor, but its practical success surpasses what I had deemed to be possible. In fact one hardly knows which most to admire, the ingenuity and the philanthropic zeal of the teacher, or the wonderful progress and attainments of the pupils. Already from distant States is heard the voice of inquiry and approval; and I trust that our own successive Legislatures will continue to cherish with the kindest care this latest of the benevolent institutions of Massachusetts, which is opening a new world to the fettered mind and is literally teaching the dumb to speak.

I cannot close this statement of the official action of this Board, without adverting again to the high order of talent which has been so freely bestowed for the public service in one of its departments, and which should be generously remembered by the people of the Commonwealth. The Secretary, Mr. Frank B.

6

Sanborn, at the call of my predecessor, brought to his
arduous task great native ability, and the resources of
a mind well stored with varied learning and controlled
by the instincts and training of a scholar. To his
industry and research we owe much invaluable statistical information, and facts and suggestions of the
utmost importance touching the moral and economical
management of our Prisons and Jails, which will
doubtless form the basis of future legislation; and it
is to his extensive acquaintance and correspondence
that we are largely indebted for that publicity of the
proceedings of his Board in other States and foreign
lands, which has so materially enhanced the reputation and the influence of Massachusetts. My regret
at his retirement will be shared by all who believe
in judicious progress and who love humanity.

Nor can I permit the retirement of the general
agent of the Board, Dr. H. B. Wheelwright, to pass
without an expression of obligation. It does not
easily occur that for the period of eleven years a
State receives from one of its officers the benefit of so
great executive ability, coupled with so philosophic
comprehension of the subjects of investigation. With
uncommon quickness to detect the meritorious from
the undeserving, the rightful claim from the fraudulent pretext, with a knowledge of classes and cases

derived from assiduous inquiry and quickened by sagacious perception, he has long been a master of his department and a conservator to the treasury. To him we are indebted for organizing at once the new system out of the old, and for demonstrating by produced results that economy and humanity may be united in the performance of this most delicate and difficult duty of administration. The files of the Auditor and Treasurer are evidence that no accounting officer has been more punctilious. Retiring from a broad field of labor in which he has, by untiring industry, kept the exceptional classes from vicious overgrowth, saving to the Commonwealth each year an amount which, under an administrator less faithful or intelligent, would have proved a heavy pecuniary burden, he has left on the records of the Board enduring proofs of his efficiency and integrity.

THE PHYSICAL SCIENCES—LOUIS AGASSIZ.

I regret to have to communicate to you the resignation by Mr. William Gray of the position of a trustee of the Museum of Comparative Zoölogy. The act incorporating the trustees, (chapter two hundred and eight of the acts of 1859,) provides that "the places of Louis Agassiz and William Gray, whenever the same or either of them shall become vacant, shall be filled by a concurrent vote of the Senate and House of Representatives." The retirement of Mr. Gray from a place in which for nine years he has rendered such eminent services to the cause of education marks a point in the history of this institution, at which it may be neither unprofitable nor uninteresting briefly to review what have been its means and opportunities of usefulness, and what its improvement of them.

Since a period so recent as to be within the remembrance of all of us, the line of distinction between what were called the learned professions and the other avocations of society has been in great measure effaced; or, perhaps I should rather say, various other avocations have come to share with these professions a degree of responsibility for the common welfare such as was not formerly recognized. With the development of manufactures and mines, of commerce, of railroads and telegraphs, a higher capacity for command, a clearer discretion in its exercise and a more extensive education for its duties, have become necessary. The various establishments of instruction in the natural sciences (of which the Museum of Comparative Zoölogy is the most conspicuous) owe their development to this cause; and, in turn, they themselves foster and promote the very cause in which they had their origin. To conduct successfully almost any great manufacturing establishment to-day requires from young men the practical application of a degree of scientific knowledge which fifty years ago was possessed only by a few and was acquired by them only as the result of long lives of study. And the same may be said concerning many other employments of our time. The Institute of Technology, at Boston, to whose funds the State has largely contributed, the Lawrence Scientific School at Cambridge, and the Worcester School of Industrial Science, founded on a liberal scale by private munificence, are landmarks in the same line of progress. Although the first of these has been in operation less than three years, its influence is already felt by the whole community. The last, though not yet fully developed, is rapidly approaching a position of general importance, adding in its system of instruction a department for the practical application of the mechanic arts,—a purpose which it is interesting to note was contemplated by Congress in its grant of public lands which we have applied to endow the Agricultural College at Amherst. It would be pleasing in this connection to set forth details of the progress and condition of all these various institutions; but that would lead me into a dissertation beyond my purpose in speaking of the Museum at Cambridge.

When Professor Agassiz came to this country twenty-two years ago, he at once began to form a collection to illustrate the history of the animal kingdom, and on this expended all his private means and put himself under large pecuniary obligations beyond them. He accepted and held the office of a professor in the Lawrence Scientific School of Harvard College, but the pecuniary aid which the college could afford . him was very little; and the only store-house for all his collections, including those gathered from his expeditions to Florida and to the great northern lakes, was a small and ill-built wooden structure, part of which he was obliged to devote to rooms for his students, artists and assistants. This in 1856 was the condition of the nucleus of the present Museum.

But in that year the magnificent private subscription of twenty-five hundred names for the publication of his work on Natural History was made; and in 1857 the first volume was issued. The Museum was greatly increased by the specimens needed to illustrate this work; and at last public attention was attracted to its importance, and a private subscription which yielded over $72,000 was made in aid of it, the Legislature at the same time voting an appropriation of $100,000 to be paid from sales of the Back Bay Lands. This appropriation was in singular conformity with that provision of the constitution (part 2, chapter 5, section 2,) which made it " the duty of legislatures and magistrates " " to cherish the interests of literature and the sciences and all seminaries of them," and " to encourage private societies and public institutions " " for the promotion," among other things enumerated, " of a *Natural History* of the country." On the death of Mr. Francis C. Gray, which occurred about this time, the Museum received the munificent legacy of $50,000, and in accordance with his request took its present name of the Museum of Comparative Zoölogy; and the act of incorporation was passed, from which I have already quoted. In 1861, the Legislature voted an additional appropriation of $20,000 ; in 1863, the sum of $10,000 was voted for the publication of illustrated catalogues ; in 1867, $10,000 for the arrangement of the great Brazilian collections ; and in 1868 a further appropriation of $75,000, to be paid in three annual instalments of $25,000 each, conditional upon the raising of the same annual amount by private subscription. I had the pleasure of signing the warrant for the payment of the first instalment on the last day of the year which has just expired.

Excluding from consideration this last grant, the whole sum which the State has contributed to the Museum during the last ten years is $140,000 ; and

during the same time it has derived from legacies and
private gifts about $175,000; to all which must be
added, what is hardly capable of being definitely computed, the sum spent meanwhile by Professor Agassiz
from his own earnings and the tuition fees of his students, (which last, however, he has almost always re-
mitted to them.) The investment of this total sum of
about $315,000 has been substantially as follows: in
a permanent fund, $150,000; in the building, $75,000;
in the scientific expedition to the Amazon, more than
$30,000, the whole of which was given for that special
purpose by one individual, Mr. Nathaniel Thayer, of
widely known liberality and public spirit; for the
purchase of collections, of glass, alcohol and other
material, upwards of $60,000. During the same time
there have been received as income of invested funds
upwards of $70,000, which have been expended in
increasing and arranging the collections.

If, now, in behalf of the State and the community
we should undertake to strike a balance sheet, as a
merchant would do in his business, and compute what
has been gained to the public from this pecuniary
investment, some of our gains might be enumerated
as follows.

First. It has secured in Massachusetts larger and
more complete collections in several grand depart-

ments of natural history than the British Museum or the Jardin des Plantes have acquired from a century of liberal government patronage.

Second. In the arrangement of these collections, even to the limited extent to which the pecuniary resources of the Museum have enabled it to be carried, it has presented to the scientific world a plan of classification and exhibition more admirable than was ever before attempted or even designed, its grand outline being to illustrate the plan of creation so far as it lies within the comprehension of the human mind.

Third. It has educated gratuitously a large part of the younger class of naturalists in this country, who now in turn are teaching in the schools and colleges of almost every State, and some of whom have already attained a reputation not limited to America; and in educating them it has afforded greater facilities for the comprehension of their special subjects of study than they could have obtained anywhere else in the world.

Fourth. It has supplied free of charge to every trustworthy scientific man in America or Europe, who chose to apply, all the specimens in its possession for his free investigation,—a purpose never before carried out on such a scale by any Museum.

Fifth. It has given courses of lectures every year, free of charge, on the higher branches of Natural His-

tory, to all teachers of either private or public schools
who should choose to attend them.

Sixth. It has published a series of valuable scientific works and supplied material for many more.

And lastly, it has secured to the United States one
who without contest is conceded to be not second to
any philosophic zoölogist now living; who during
his residence of twenty years with us has given to
scientific pursuits in this country a new and previously unknown impulse; has made the scientific attainments and achievements of Americans known and
respected abroad; and has concentrated in Massachusetts unequalled facilities and incitements for this
class of studies.

*All which has been accomplished at a cost less than
that of a small cotton mill.*

I have deemed it proper to invite attention to this
recent feature of our system of education. It has
been the most agreeable of my official duties to give
frequent attendance at the schools, to become familiar
with their wants, and to encourage the adoption of all
unquestionable methods of advancing their influence.
And, in retiring from that relation of duty to the institutions of learning which the Constitution imposes
upon the Executive, I take special pleasure in commending to public respect the example of the men and

the seminaries that have been pioneers in adapting our system to our necessity. The five classical colleges of the Commonwealth are secure upon permanent endowments and certain patronage. The discipline and culture of their rich and varied instruction is imparted to constantly increasing numbers within their walls, and diffuses its beneficence over all classes. But, for the intense life of our time, for an age of commerce, mechanism and all the arts, yet other and specific policies and adaptations of education are needed. The work of supplying them has begun, and no degree of public or private favor in carrying on the work can exceed the demand.

HOOSAC TUNNEL CONTRACT.

The Legislature of 1868, by chapter 333 of its acts, authorized the Governor and Council to contract for the whole work of constructing the Hoosac Tunnel, limiting the price to five millions of dollars and the time to seven years, with satisfactory guarantees, and further providing that one million of dollars should be withheld from payment until the work should be finished and accepted. A supplemental act, chapter 350, modified the former by authorizing the expenditure of two hundred and fifty thousand dollars, (taken from the five millions,) upon the continued prosecution of the enterprise under existing contracts and in paying off present liabilities, and by further providing that under any contract for the completion of the Tunnel twenty per centum should be reserved in the payment by instalments. This action of the legislature was on the eleventh of June, and, immediately after the prorogation of that body, the Governor and Council adopted measures for advertising for proposals. The bids were opened on the first of September. It will be seen by an examination of the statement which I have the honor herewith to transmit to the General Court that these were twelve in number, of which five only came within the amount remaining at the disposal of the Governor and Council, (four million seven hundred and fifty thousand dollars,) the others exceeding that sum.

In considering these proposals for the contract, the first question which arose, was, what should be deemed "satisfactory guarantees." Several parties were ready to offer a bond with sureties; but, for various reasons, too obvious to need repeating, and especially in consideration of the long period which any bond must cover, I deemed it my duty to decline every such offer. It only remained to require an actual deposit of approved public securities of satisfactory amount. To establish this amount involved the

exercise of individual discretion, and to some extent
the adoption of an apparently arbitrary standard.
After much reflection and consultation with the Council, I settled in the conclusion that the amount to be
deposited should be five hundred thousand dollars.
It seemed to me that such a sum in hand, together
with the retention of twenty per centum in making
payments, ought to be accepted as satisfactory guarantees against the risk of an abandonment of the work
by contractors, which would probably be more immi-
nent in its early than in its later stages. Another and
important element in the estimate of guarantees, and
primary to every other, was to be found in the character and fitness of the men who should be admitted
to the contract. In my judgment the requirement of
so large a deposit would quite certainly exclude all
persons who could not command public confidence,
and would keep the undertaking from the hands of
mere adventurers and speculators. I believe that such
a result has been attained. Nor was it in my mind
any objection to the demand of a positive and large
security that it might involve the declinature of the
lower bids and an approach to the highest; for the
economy of a State, as of an individual, may lie in the
acceptance of the larger price coupled with the greater
certainty of fulfilment. The contract finally made was

with the third in the order of the bidders, and was in accordance with the guarantees required, which, modified only in form, have been substantially obtained.

The contract for the construction of the Hoosac Tunnel was executed on the twenty-fourth of December by the Governor and Council, with Walter Shanly, of Montreal, and Francis Shanly, of Toronto, Canada, for the sum of four million five hundred and ninety-four thousand two hundred and sixty-eight dollars, ($4,594,268,) to be paid in United States Treasury notes or other current funds. I herewith communicate to the legislature a copy of this contract. Before committing the Commonwealth to the agreement, its terms were examined and discussed by the Governor and Council, from day to day, for the greater part of a month, and with every aid which could be derived from experience and testimony. The contractors bring to this enterprise the advantages of large experience in railroad construction and mining, of distinguished reputation in the community where they reside, and of command of financial resources, themselves stimulated by confident expectations of profit. They have already commenced the preparation; and one of them at least will transfer his residence to the field of operations.

For the details of the contract, I refer to the instru-

ment itself, but a few of its provisions demand specific
mention. It is agreed that no sum whatever shall
become due to the contractors until after work to the
amount of five hundred thousand dollars shall have
been performed by them and approved by the Governor and Council. It will be readily perceived that
for the period of two-thirds of a year, more or less, and
through that stage which will probably be decisive of
the result, they are to work without cost or recourse
to the Commonwealth. Again, the reserve of a half
million is equivalent to twenty per centum of two and
a half millions, or almost five-ninths of the entire price,
which by the provision for reservation under the law
alone would not be attained in a less period than two
years and a half. The first of the two acts referred
to required the withholding of a million dollars until
after the completion of the Tunnel; the second required
only the reservation of twenty per centum, which
under the present contract would amount at the end
to only about nine hundred thousand dollars; and the
second act changed and so far repealed the first. But
the contract is in careful conformity to the intention
of both acts, specifically withholding the twenty per
centum on each of the instalments, and further providing that the full sum of one million dollars shall
be kept back until the completion of the whole work.

The statute extended the time for the entire construction to June, 1875 ; but the contract limits it to March, 1874, within the discretion of the Governor and Council to grant a further extension of six months. It is also made a part of the agreement that at any time, with three months' notice, the Governor and Council may terminate the entire contract. Without other statement of the details, I invite the attention of the legislature to the whole document, which is the result of the utmost care and deliberation of the Governor and Council to whom the legislature assigned this grave and responsible trust.

I regard the completion of this enterprise as already assured within the terms of the contract. It is proper then to state what in that event will be the total cost of the Railroad and Tunnel. Excluding interest, the whole amount that will have been expended on the Railroad from Greenfield to North Adams, including also the purchase of the Southern Vermont Railroad, according to the tables herewith sent to the Legislature, will be one million six hundred and sixty-six thousand two hundred and fifty dollars ($1,666,250). The amount already laid out upon the Tunnel itself and exterior works properly chargeable to it, including the payment for some work now approaching completion under existing contracts, is three million two thousand one hundred and seventy-six dollars ($3,002,176). The amount to be paid the Messrs. Shanly under the contract upon the final construction of the Tunnel is four million five hundred and ninety-four thousand two hundred and sixty-eight dollars ($4,594,268). The result therefore may be stated as follows :

Total cost of Tunnel including track,	$7,596,444	00
Total cost of Railway, . . .	1,666,250	00
Total cost of Tunnel, and Railway,	———	
fifty miles in length, . . .	$9,262,694	00

If now there be added the cost of the other railroads connecting with this, and together with it constituting the through line from Boston to Troy, one hundred and eighty-nine miles in length, the result will show a united capital of not far from sixteen millions of dollars ($16,000,000). In this statement I make only a reasonable discount for that portion of the Vermont and Massachusetts Railroad diverging from Greenfield to Brattleborough. This line has already nearly sixty miles of double track, the most favorable gradients, ample facilities at deep water, a large real estate, a profitable local business, and a command, so soon as the mountain shall be pierced, of the far-reaching connections which ally the manufactures and commerce of

8

the East to the granaries of the West. I never have
doubted, and I do not now doubt, that this whole line
will be worth all it will have cost,—worth it directly,
and for business,—worth it twice over indirectly, by
developing now latent capacities and resources of this
progressive community of more than a million and a
quarter of souls, and by adding rapidly to the tax-
able property of the Commonwealth. I confidently
look forward to the day, now not distant, when the
four railways connecting Troy with Boston, the lakes
by nearest transit with the sea, shall be consolidated
in the interest of commerce, under one seal and one
control. The three corporations which, by the contract made in 1863, must pay to the State the tribute
of twenty per centum of all revenue received from
traffic passing through the Tunnel or over any part
of the Troy and Greenfield Railway, will then have
a strong inducement for such an arrangement; the
interest of the Commonwealth will favor it; the
irresistible laws of trade and transport will demand
it. In the negotiations and adjustments of that
future day I can readily foresee that the Commonwealth need not be largely, if at all, the loser on
its costly enterprise, regarded only as a pecuniary
investment. And even if the treasury shall not
then recover the whole of its disbursement, more

than an equivalent will be received by the people in the economy of their commerce and the increase of their wealth. As I had the honor to say in my annual message to the Legislature in 1867, the value of great public works, conceived in the necessities of States, looking not to the specific returns of remunerative interest for a single year or a limited number of years, but rather to the compensation of internal commerce through successive generations, cannot be computed by the rules that govern private investment based on the promise of immediate profit. The finance of individuals comes within the limitations of present and personal interest; the investment of Commonwealths looks for a return in their complete development and in their enduring destiny. So have judged the great commercial and manufacturing States of New York and Pennsylvania; and so they have builded their material success on partial forgetfulness of immediate profit and on confidence in the longer and grander future. Massachusetts cannot afford to cherish a policy less broad than that which has conducted them to prosperity and greatness.

Senators and Representatives:

In administering the office of Chief Magistrate I have been filled with constantly increasing respect for the institutions of the Commonwealth which for a period of three years it has been my high privilege to guard with executive care. Not any citizen, so well as they who from this post of observation have been called to keep constant watch of the whole field, can grasp in thought and affection the history, the growth, the felicity of the people of Massachusetts. In the discharge of my duty to be diligent in aid of their material wealth and power, of their schools and charities, and from the fountain of mercy to temper justice, it has been my opportunity to learn how strong, intelligent, just and humane is the community in which we live. To have been permitted to serve in official station a State so organized under forms of the highest culture and humanity, may justly be regarded as honor; but in private station there is honor also in every well meant exertion of the citizen to contribute to the welfare of all. In passing from one of these relations to the other, I unite with you in commending our Commonwealth to the continued favor of the God of our Fathers.

ALEXANDER H. BULLOCK.

www.ingramcontent.com/pod-product-compliance
Lightning Source LLC
Chambersburg PA
CBHW031749090426
42739CB00008B/938